Walkthrough

This is the front cover.

What do you think this story is going to be about?

Let's read the title: 'A Flash of Lightning'.

Do you like it when there's a storm with thunder and lightning?

Walkthrough

This is the back cover.

Can you show me the blurb?

Let's read it together.

What do you think the Fantastic Forest creatures would do when they saw that a storm was coming?

Walkthrough

This is the title page.

Can you see the title again here?

Let's read it again.

Who can you see in the picture? (*Dash the unicorn and her friend*)

How do you think they feel about the lightning?

 **Walkthrough**

What's going on in this picture? (*there's a flash of lightning*)

Can you see the word 'flash' on the page?

Flash!

There was a big flash of lightning. It lit up the sky.

2

 Observe and Prompt

Word Recognition

- Encourage the children to split 'lightning' into two syllables. Remind them how to pronounce the 'igh' trigraph.

- Check that the children use their decoding skills to read 'flash', sounding out and blending the letters all through the word.

- Check that the children can read the high frequency words 'there' and 'was' on sight. Prompt them if necessary.

 Use these pointers to gain evidence for AF1.

FLASH!

3

 Observe and Prompt

Language Comprehension

- Ask the children how they feel when there is a storm with lightning. How do they think the Fantastic Forest creatures will feel?

- Check that the children read the text with appropriate expression.

Ⓐ Use this question to gain evidence for AF6.

Walkthrough

Who can you see here? (*Big Eyes the owl*)

Do you think he likes the storm?

What do you think he wants to do?

Big Eyes looked up.

"A big storm is coming," he said.

"I will stay here, in my tree."

4

👁 Observe and Prompt

Word Recognition

- If the children struggle with the words 'looked' and 'coming', encourage them to use their decoding skills to tackle the words as far as possible. Show them how to split 'coming' into two syllables to help them read it, and model reading the words for them if necessary.

- Check that the children are using their decoding skills to tackle 'storm', 'stay' and 'tree', sounding out and blending the letter sounds through each word if necessary.

4

5

 Observe and Prompt

Language Comprehension

- Ask the children if they think Big Eyes is scared of the storm. Would they be scared, if they were outside in a storm at night?

A Use this question to gain evidence for AF6.

 **Walkthrough**

Does Binks the elf look happy about the storm?

What's she doing? *(hiding in her bed)*

"I don't like lightning," said Binks.

She hid in her bed.

6

 Observe and Prompt

Word Recognition

- Check that the children can read the high frequency words 'don't' and 'said' on sight. Prompt them if necessary.

- Check that the children are using their decoding skills to read the other words, and remind them how to tackle 'lightning' by splitting it into syllables if necessary.

 Use this pointer to gain evidence for AF1.

6

7

 Observe and Prompt

Language Comprehension

- Ask the children why they think Binks decided to hide in her bed.

(A) Use this question to gain evidence for AF3.

 **Walkthrough**

Do you think Hector likes the storm?

What makes you think that?

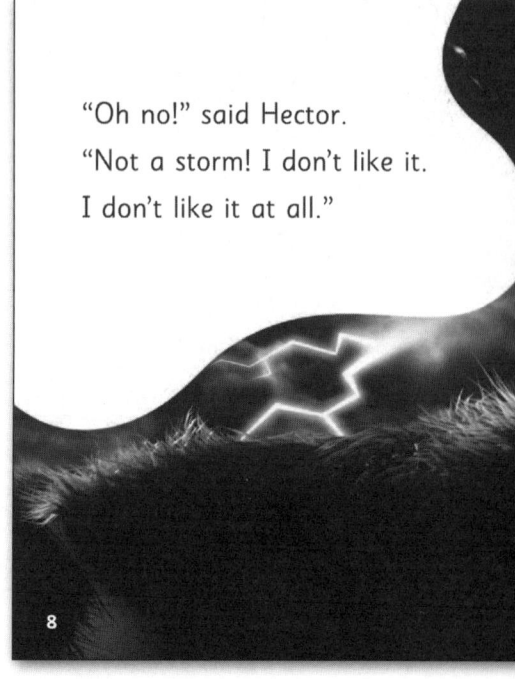

"Oh no!" said Hector.
"Not a storm! I don't like it.
I don't like it at all."

8

Observe and Prompt

Word Recognition

- Prompt the children if necessary to split the word 'Hector' into syllables and sound out and blend the letters all through each syllable to read the word.

- Check that the children can recognise and read the high frequency words 'said', 'don't' and 'like' on sight.

(A) Use this pointer to gain evidence for AF1.

9

Observe and Prompt

Language Comprehension

- Ask the children how they think Hector is feeling, and why.

- Encourage them to read the words Hector says with expression, to show how he feels.

 **Walkthrough**

Do you think Boo the monster likes the lightning?

Do you think monsters like it when it's dark?

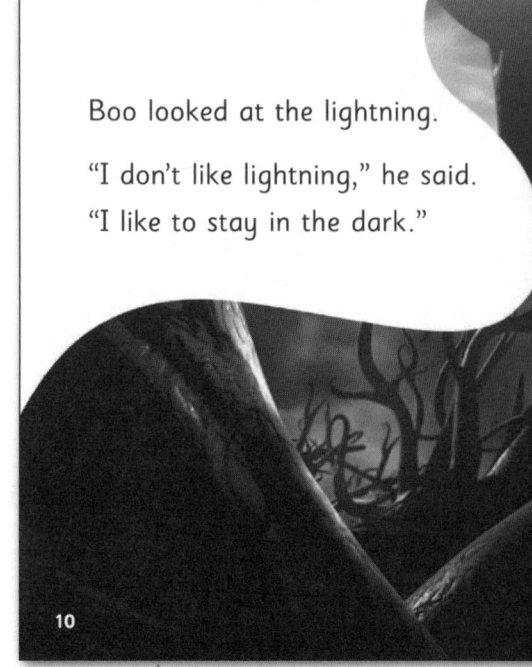

Boo looked at the lightning.

"I don't like lightning," he said.
"I like to stay in the dark."

10

 Observe and Prompt

Word Recognition

- Encourage the children to use their decoding skills to tackle 'stay' and 'dark', sounding out and blending the letters all through the word if necessary.

- If the children struggle with 'looked', 'lightning' and 'don't', model how to read these words.

11

Language Comprehension

- Ask the children why they think a monster might want to stay in the dark. (*E.g. the dark can be scary and monsters like scary things; or you can hide in the dark and creep up on people to give them a shock ...*)

A Use this question to gain evidence for AF3.

 **Walkthrough**

Why do you think Dash and her friend are hiding in the cave?

Would this be a good place to go to watch the storm?

"Oh no!" said Dash.
"The rain is coming."

She hid in the cave with her friend.

12

 Observe and Prompt

Word Recognition

- If the children struggle with 'coming' and 'friend', model how to read these words for them.

- Check that the children can read the long vowel 'a' sound in both 'rain' and 'cave'.

13

👁 Observe and Prompt

Language Comprehension

- Ask the children why Dash might be worried about the rain coming. (e.g. *She can't fly when her wings are wet.*)

- Check that the children can read the text with appropriate pace and expression, especially Dash's words.

- Ask the children to predict (or remember) if any of the Fantastic Forest creatures likes storms.

 **Walkthrough**

Do you think Gog the giant likes storms?

What makes you think that?

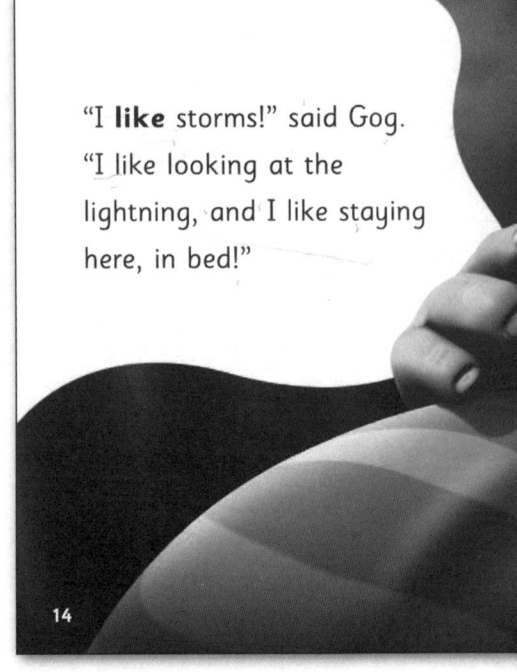

"I **like** storms!" said Gog.
"I like looking at the
lightning, and I like staying
here, in bed!"

14

 Observe and Prompt

Word Recognition

Encourage the children to split the words 'looking',
'lightning' and 'staying' into syllables and use their
decoding skills to read each syllable.

 Use this pointer to gain evidence for AF1.

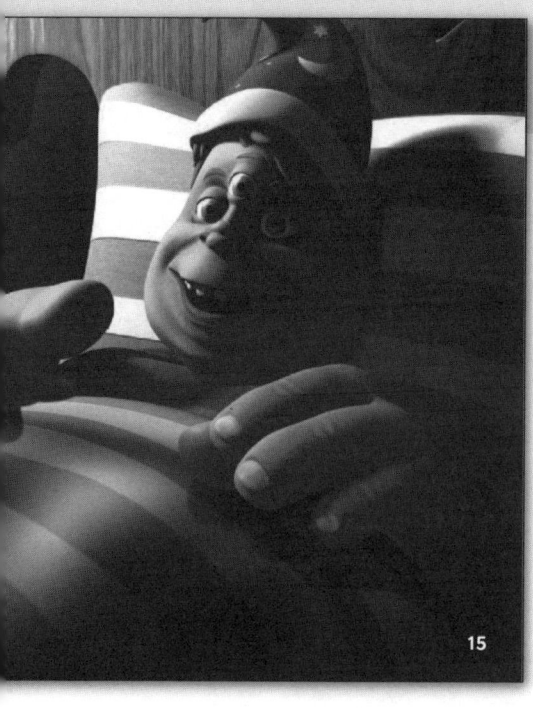

15

Language Comprehension

- Ask the children if they agree with Gog about storms. Have they ever enjoyed being warm and cosy inside when the weather is bad?

- Check that the children are reading with appropriate pace and expression, especially for the direct speech. Draw their attention if necessary to the exclamation marks and bold text, and model how to read the text appropriately.

Walkthrough

This is a quiz page. It's got some sentences that are split into two halves. We have to read them and match the two halves of each sentence.

 Observe and prompt

Word Recognition

- Check that the children are using their decoding skills to read the words.

- If the children struggle with 'coming', remind them to split it into two syllables to help read it.